VERSIONS
GUITAR
TIC TRANSCRIPTIONS
NOTES AND TABLATURE

BEATLES FOR SALE

"Rock and Roll Music" has been omitted from this publication due to licensing restrictions.

Music transcriptions by Ron Piccione and Bill LaFleur

ISBN 978-1-61780-460-1

HAL•LEONARD®
CORPORATION

7777 W. BLUEMOUND RD. P.O. BOX 13819 MILWAUKEE, WI 53213

Visit Hal Leonard Online at
www.halleonard.com

CONTENTS

No Reply

Words and Music by John Lennon and Paul McCartney

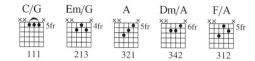

C/G   Em/G   A   Dm/A   F/A

Verse
Moderately ♩ = 124

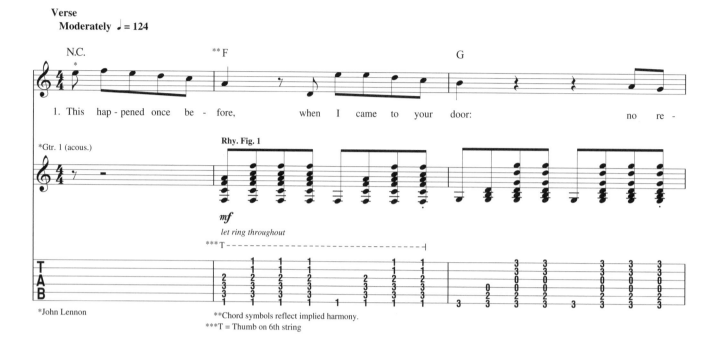

1. This hap-pened once be-fore, when I came to your door: no re-

*Gtr. 1 (acous.)

*John Lennon
**Chord symbols reflect implied harmony.
***T = Thumb on 6th string

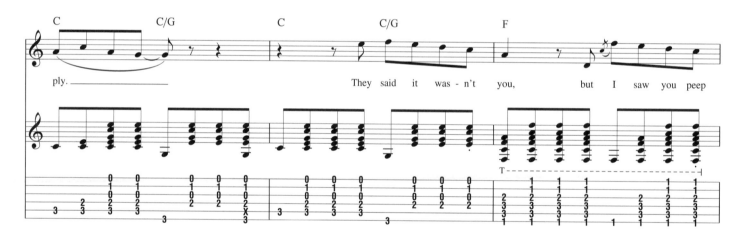

ply. They said it was-n't you, but I saw you peep

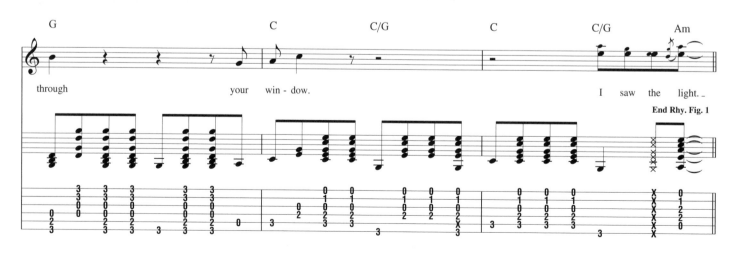

through your win-dow. I saw the light.

End Rhy. Fig. 1

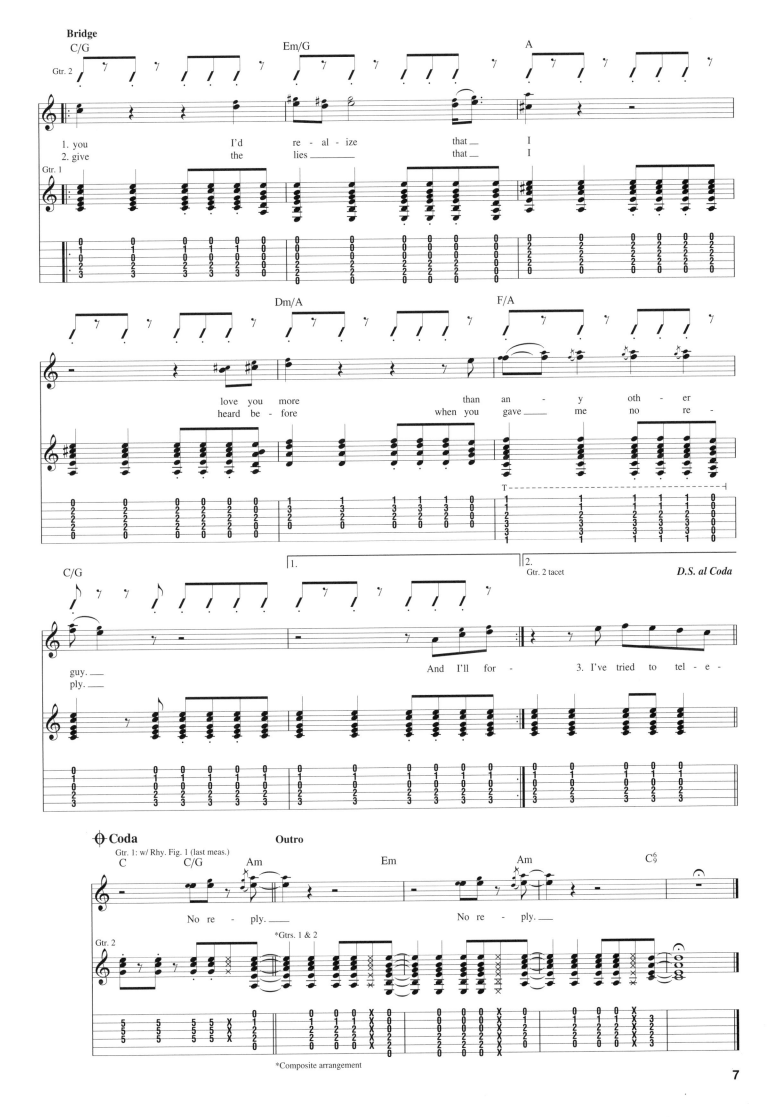

I'm a Loser

Words and Music by John Lennon and Paul McCartney

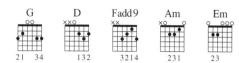

Intro
Free time

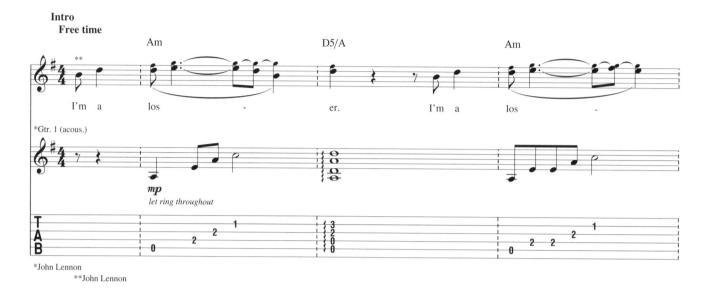

Gtr. 1 (acous.)

let ring throughout

*John Lennon
**John Lennon

Fast ♩ = 175

(cont. in slashes)

Verse

Gtr. 2 (elec.)

w/ clean tone
w/ pick & fingers
let ring throughout

***George Harrison - Two gtrs. arr. for one.

10

2nd time, Gtr. 2: w/ Riff A   2nd time, Gtr. 2: w/ Fill 3

D   Fadd9   G

My tears are fall - in' ___ like rain ___ from ___ the sky. ___
And so it's true, ___ pride comes be - fore a fall. ___

2nd time, Gtr. 2: w/ Fill 4

D   Fadd9   G

Is it ___ for her ___ or my - self ___ that ___ I cry?   I'm a los -
I'm tell - in' you ___ so ___ that you won't ___ lose ___ all.

Chorus
Gtr. 1: w/ Rhy. Fig. 2
Gtr. 2: w/ Riff B

Am   D   Am   D

- er ___ and I lost ___ some - one who's near ___ to me. I'm a los -

To Coda ⊕

G   Em   Am   Fadd9   D

- er ___ and I'm not what I ap - pear ___ to be. ___

Fill 1
Gtr. 2

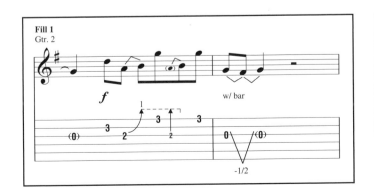

Fill 2
Gtr. 2

Baby's in Black

Words and Music by John Lennon and Paul McCartney

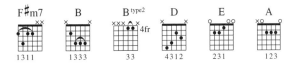

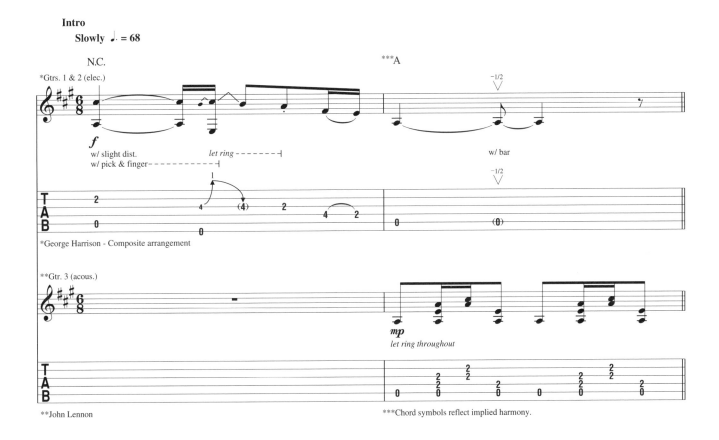

*George Harrison - Composite arrangement

**John Lennon

***Chord symbols reflect implied harmony.

†Composite arrangement

††John Lennon - full size notes, Paul McCartney - cue size notes.

feel-in' blue. Tell me, oh, _____ what can I do?

1. She _____ thinks of him _____ and so _____ she dress-es in

Verse

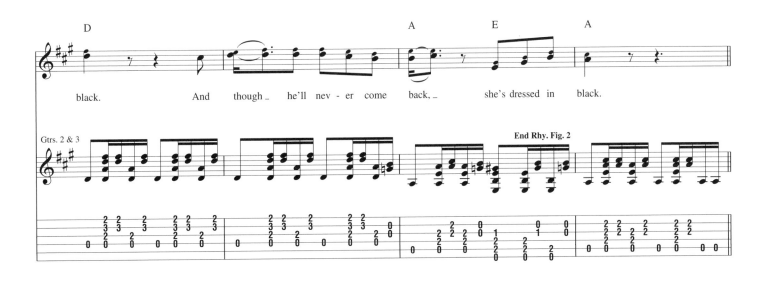

black.   And though __ he'll nev - er come back, __ she's dressed in black.

Gtrs. 2 & 3   End Rhy. Fig. 2

Chorus
Gtrs. 2 & 3: w/ Rhy. Fig. 1

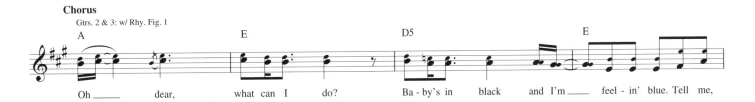

Oh _____ dear,   what can I   do?   Ba - by's in   black   and I'm ____ feel - in' blue. Tell me,

Verse
Gtrs. 2 & 3: w/ Rhy. Fig. 2

oh, _____ what can I   do?   2. I _____ think of her, _____ but

she __ thinks on - ly of   him.   And though __ it's on - ly a whim, __ she thinks of

𝄋 Bridge

him.   Oh, _____ how _____ long will it   take

Gtr. 1

Rhy. Fill 1   End Rhy. Fill 1
Gtrs. 2 & 3

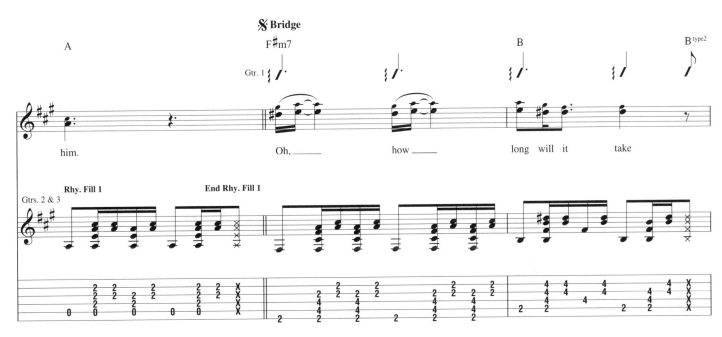

Guitar Solo

Gtr. 3: w/ Rhy. Fig. 1 (1st 5 meas.)

D.S. al Coda

Gtr. 3: w/ Rhy. Fill 1

Coda

Verse

3. She ____ thinks of him ____ and so ____ she dress-es in

Outro-Chorus

Gtr. 2: w/ Rhy. Fig. 1 (1st 5 meas.)
Gtr. 3: w/ Rhy. Fig. 1

Gtr. 1

Gtr. 2: w/ Fill 1

Gtr. 3

*Gtrs. 1 & 2

w/ pick
& finger

*Composite arrangement

I'll Follow the Sun

Words and Music by John Lennon and Paul McCartney

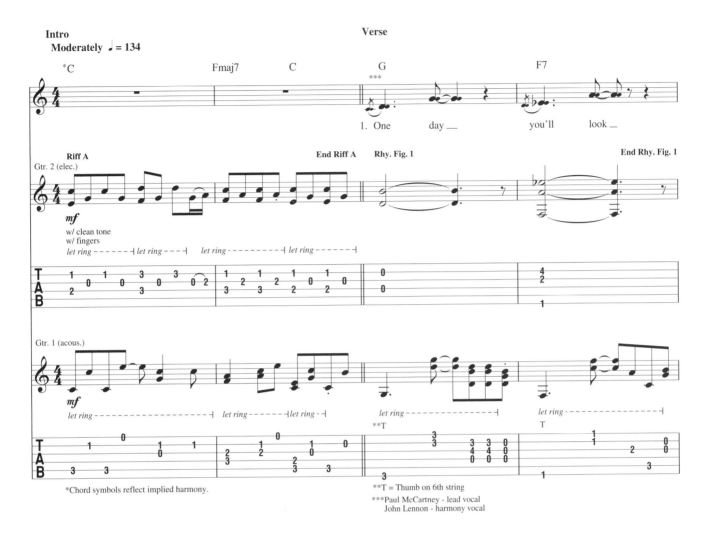

*Chord symbols reflect implied harmony.

**T = Thumb on 6th string

***Paul McCartney - lead vocal
John Lennon - harmony vocal

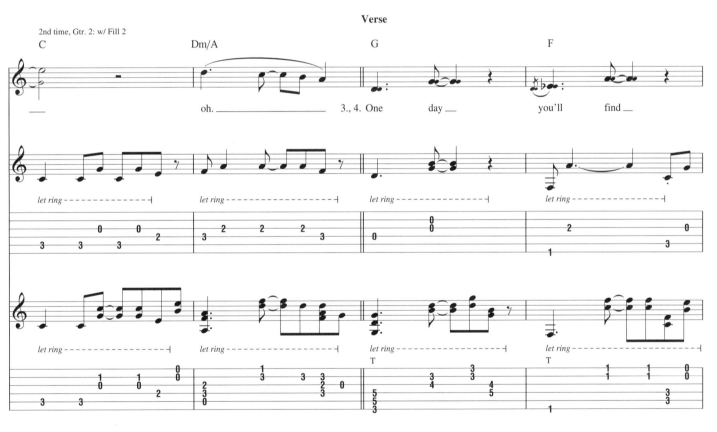

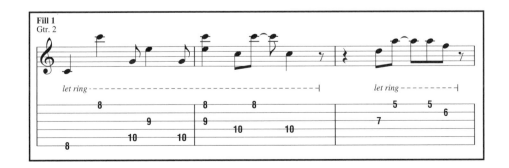

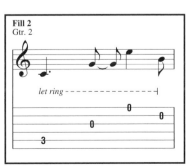

Guitar Solo/Verse

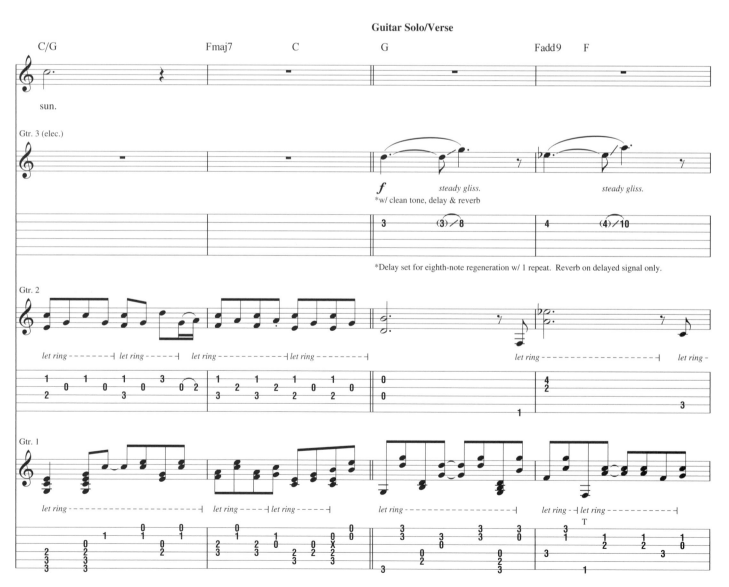

*Delay set for eighth-note regeneration w/ 1 repeat. Reverb on delayed signal only.

Yeah, to-mor-row may rain, __ so __ I'll fol-low the

D.S. al Coda

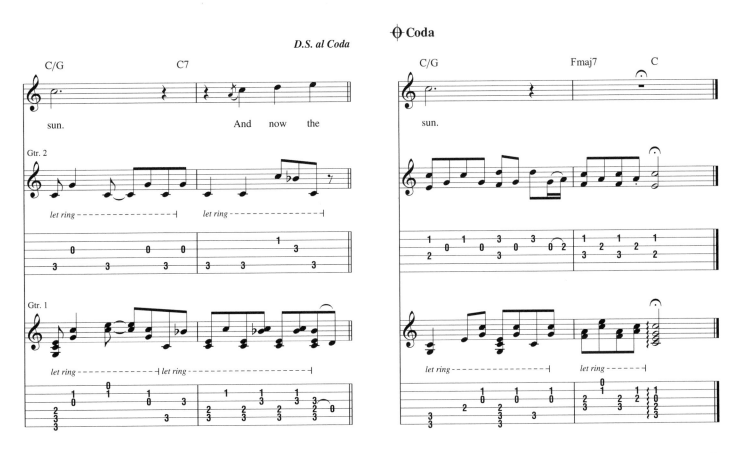

sun. And now the

⊕ Coda

sun.

Mr. Moonlight

Words and Music by Roy Lee Johnson

Intro
Free time

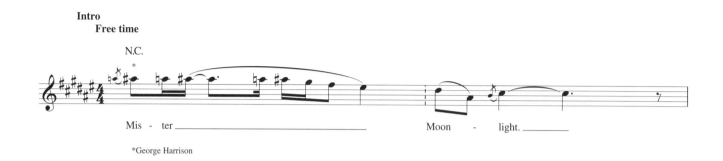

Mis - ter _____ Moon - light. _____

*George Harrison

Moderately ♩ = 125

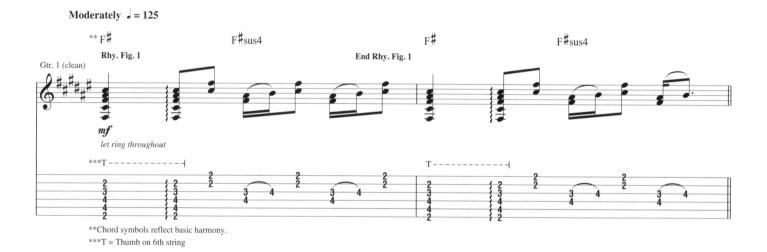

**Chord symbols reflect basic harmony.
***T = Thumb on 6th string

Verse

1. You came to me _____ one sum - mer night

Kansas City/Hey Hey Hey Hey

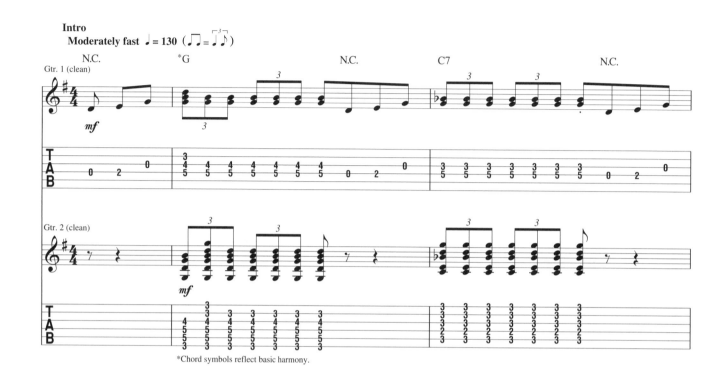

*Chord symbols reflect basic harmony.

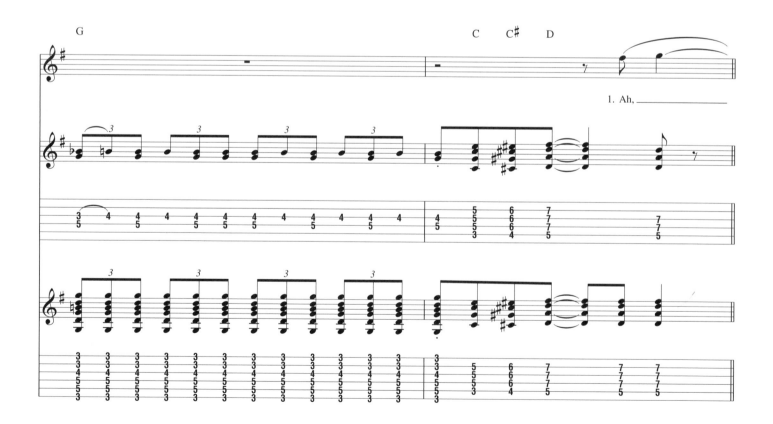

KANSAS CITY

Words and Music by Jerry Leiber and Mike Stoller

Kan - sas Cit - y, gon-na get my ba - by back home. ____ Ah, yeah, yeah. __
Kan - sas Cit - y, gon-na get my ba - by one time. ____ Ah, yeah, yeah. __

I'm go - in' to Kan - sas Cit - y, gon-na get my ba - by back home. _
I'm go - in' to Kan - sas Cit - y, gon-na get my ba - by one ____

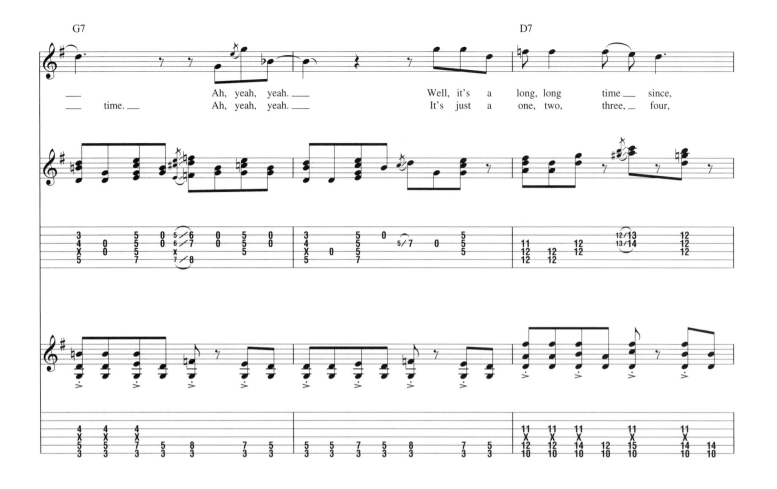

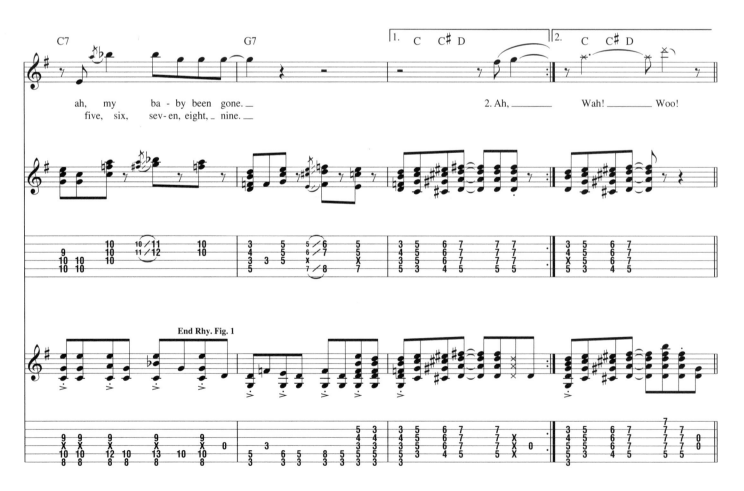

Guitar Solo

Gtr. 2: w/ Rhy. Fig. 1

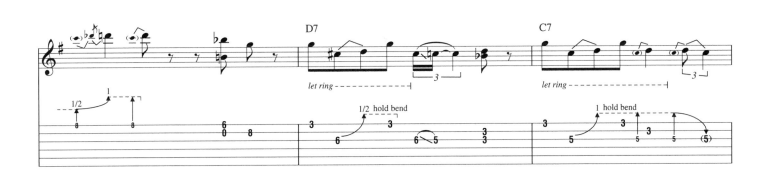

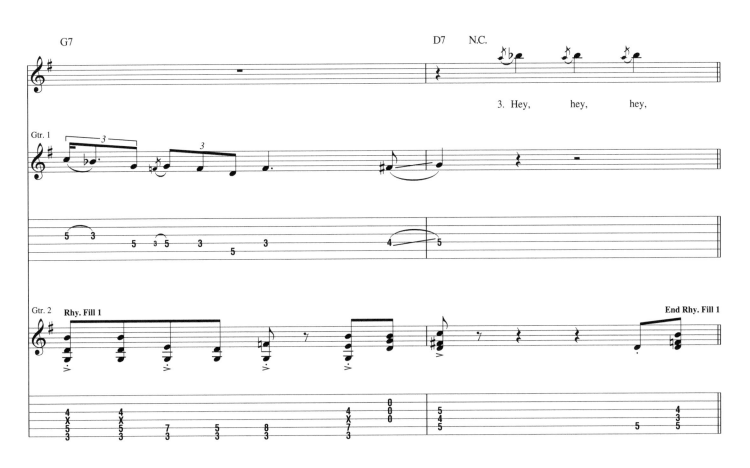

3. Hey,   hey,   hey,

HEY HEY HEY HEY
Words and Music by Richard Penniman

Verse

Outro

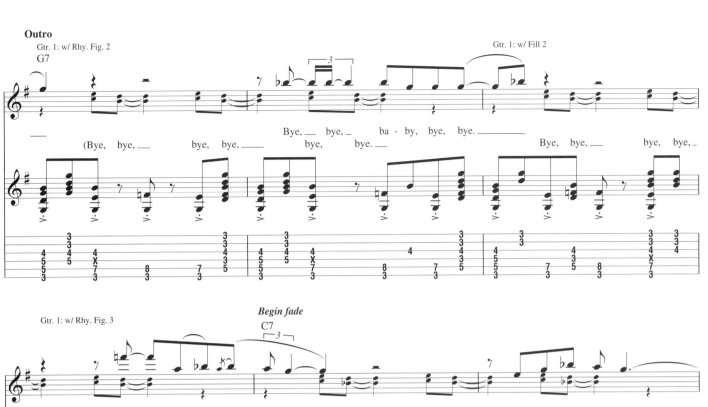

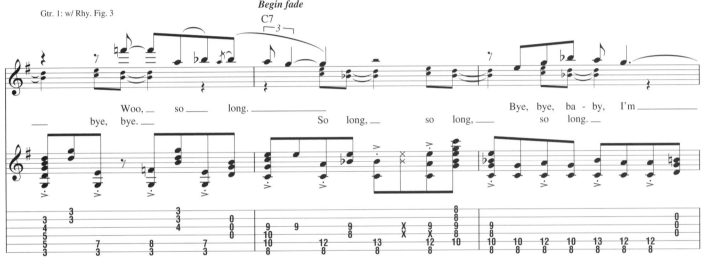

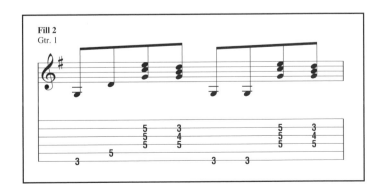

Eight Days a Week

Words and Music by John Lennon and Paul McCartney

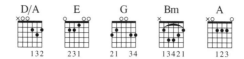

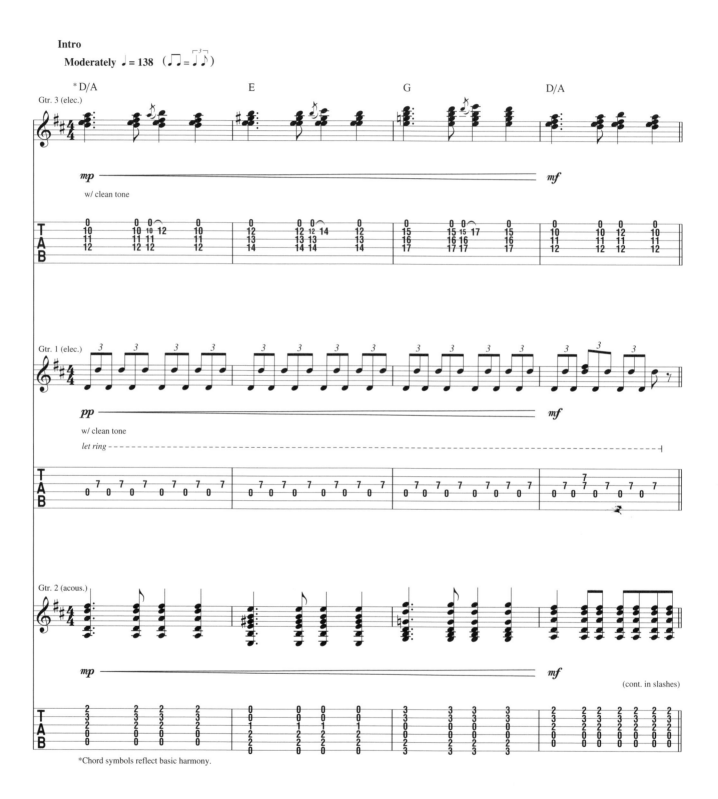

*Chord symbols reflect basic harmony.

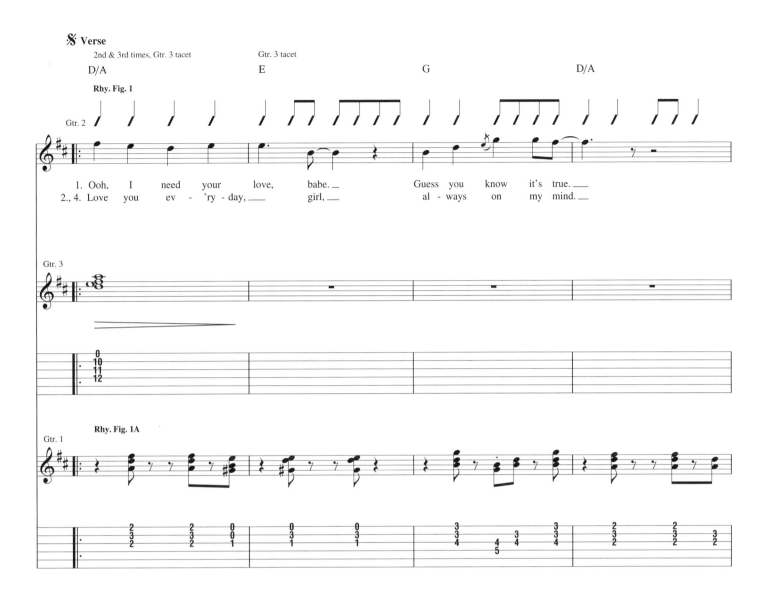

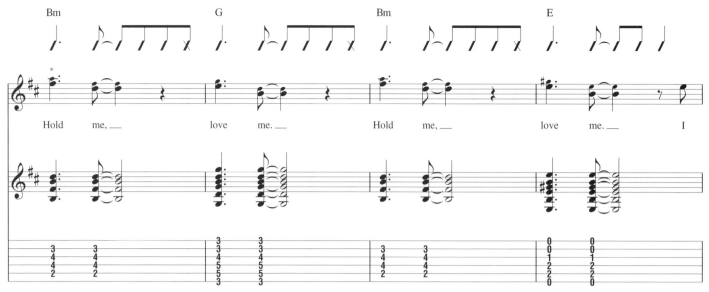

*Harm. voc. sung 2nd & 3rd times only (next 4 meas.).

To Coda ⊕

End Rhy. Fig. 1

End Rhy. Fig. 1A

Bridge

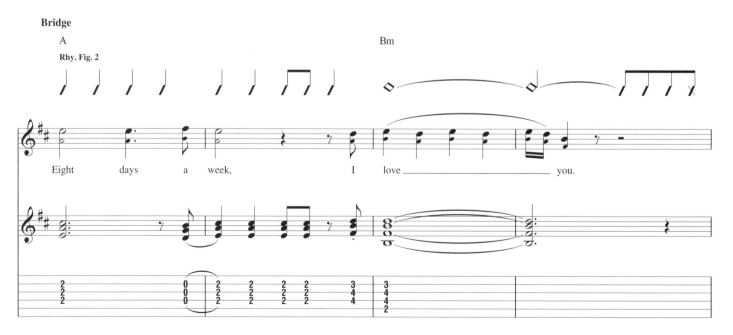

Verse

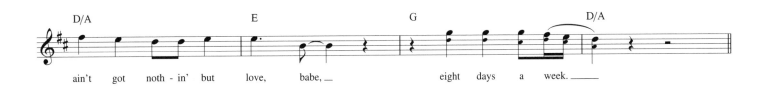

Bridge

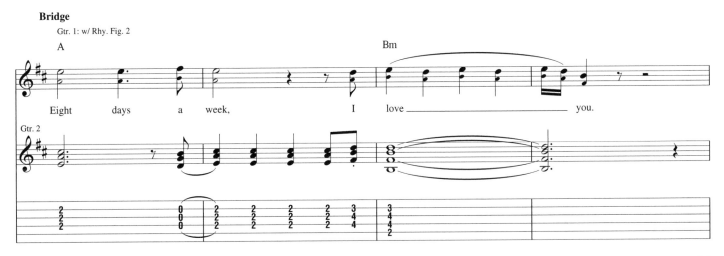

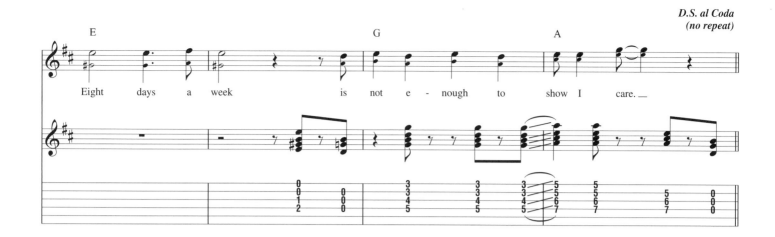

Eight days a week is not e - nough to show I care. __

Coda

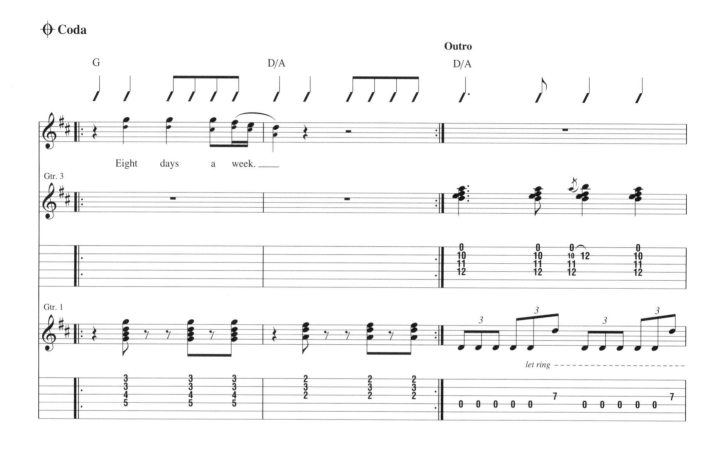

Outro

Eight days a week. __

Gtr. 3

Gtr. 1

let ring - - - - - - - - - - - - - - - - - - -

let ring -

Words of Love

Words and Music by Buddy Holly

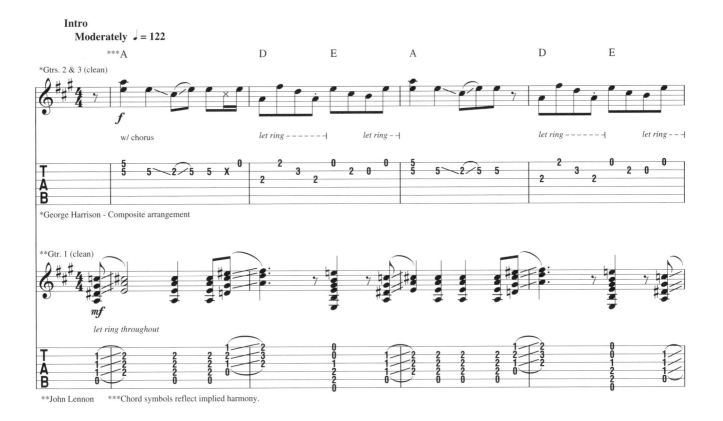

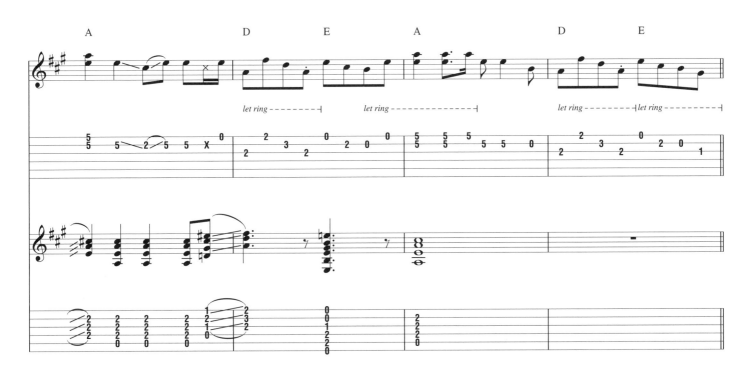

Verse

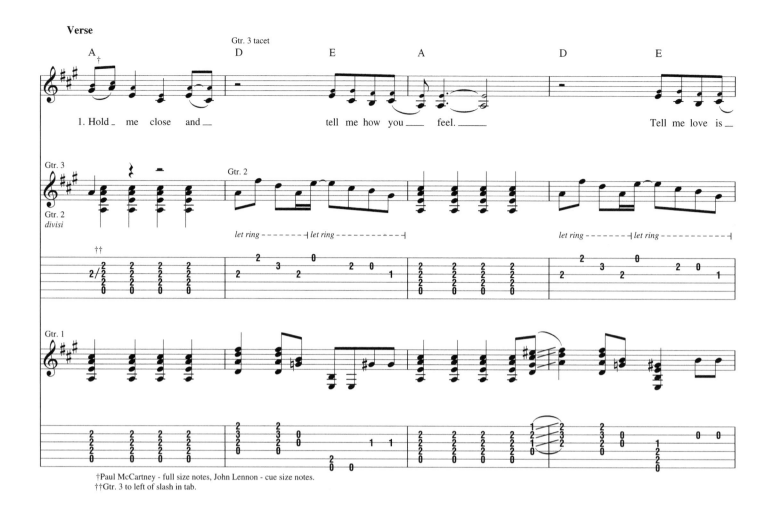

†Paul McCartney - full size notes, John Lennon - cue size notes.
††Gtr. 3 to left of slash in tab.

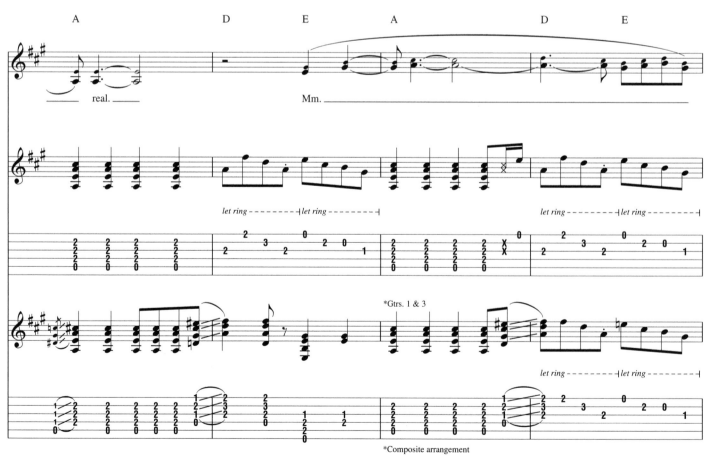

*Composite arrangement

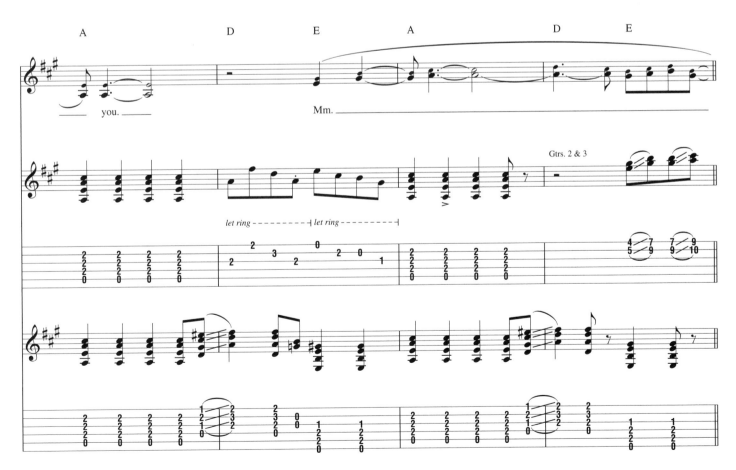

Interlude

Verse

2. Let me hear you say ___ the words I long to ___ hear. ___ Dar - ling, when you're ___

Gtr. 2

let ring

*Gtrs. 1 & 3

let ring

*Composite arrangement

___ near. ___ Mm. ___

Rhy. Fig. 1

End Rhy. Fig. 1

let ring

let ring

Honey Don't

Words and Music by Carl Lee Perkins

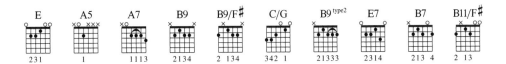

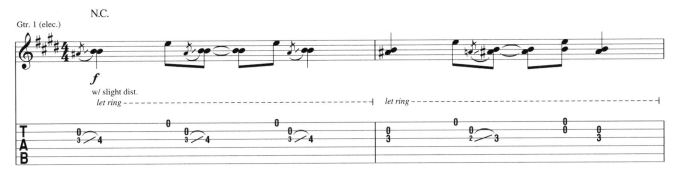

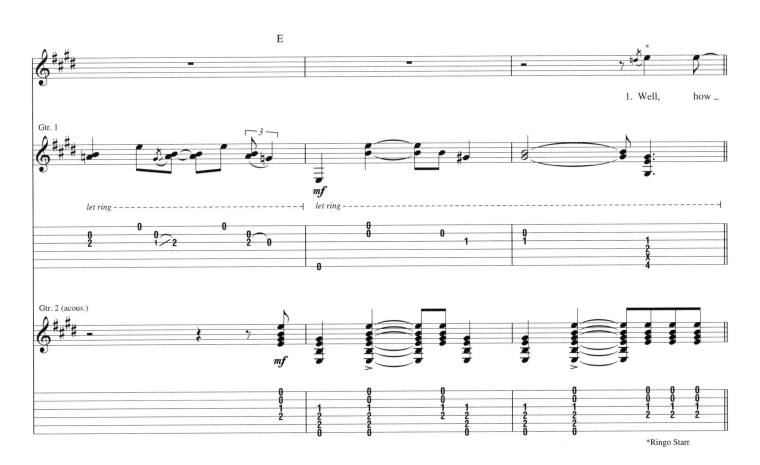

*Ringo Starr

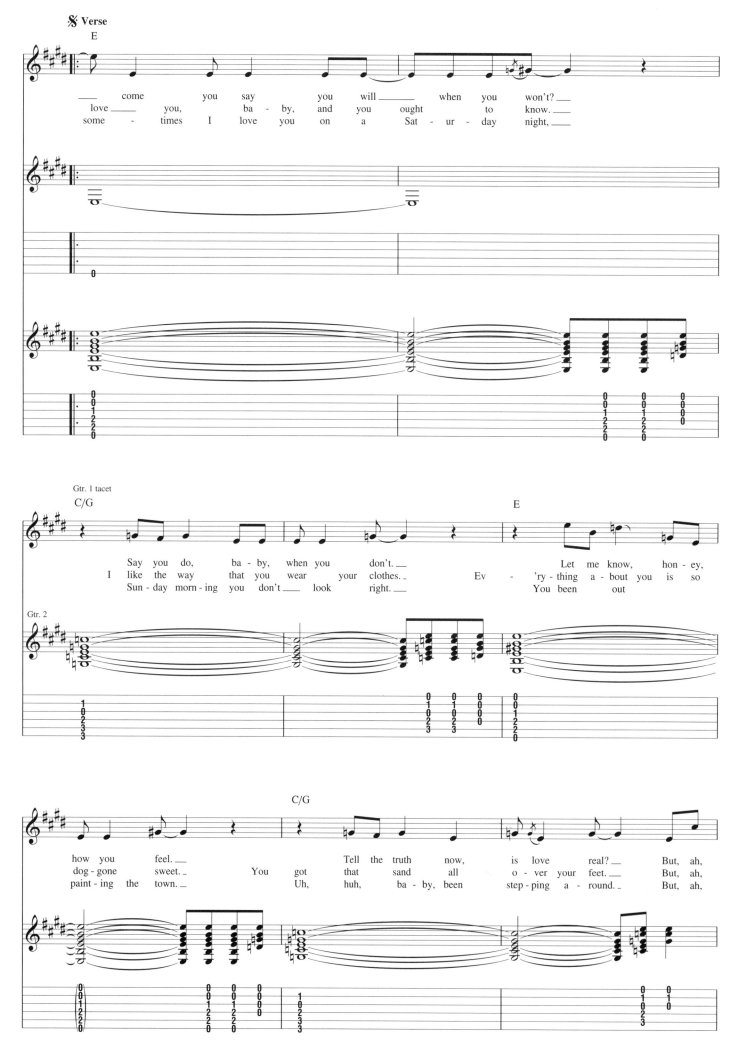

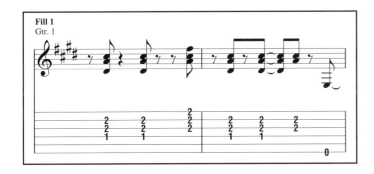
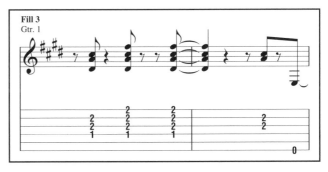

2nd time, Gtr. 1: w/ Fill 2
3rd time, Gtr. 1: w/ Fill 4

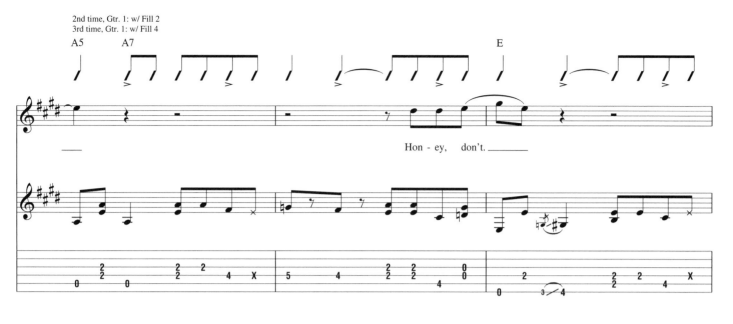

Hon - ey, don't. _____

To Coda ⊕

I say you will when you won't. ___ Ah, aw, _____ hon - ey, don't. __

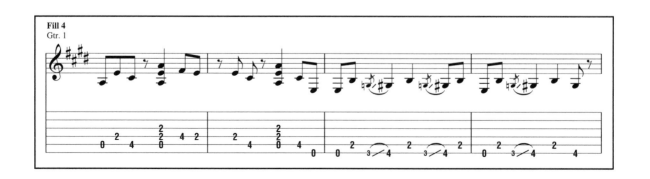

Every Little Thing

Words and Music by John Lennon and Paul McCartney

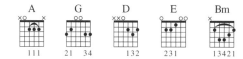

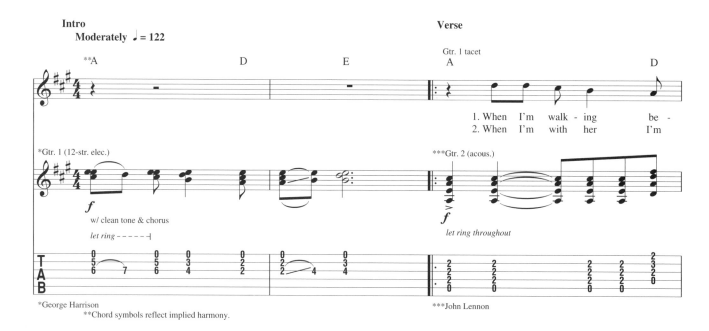

I Don't Want to Spoil the Party

Words and Music by John Lennon and Paul McCartney

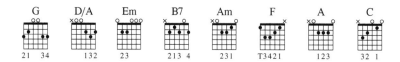

Gtr. 1: Drop D tuning:
(low to high) D-A-D-G-B-E

*George Harrison

**John Lennon

***Chord symbols reflect implied harmony.

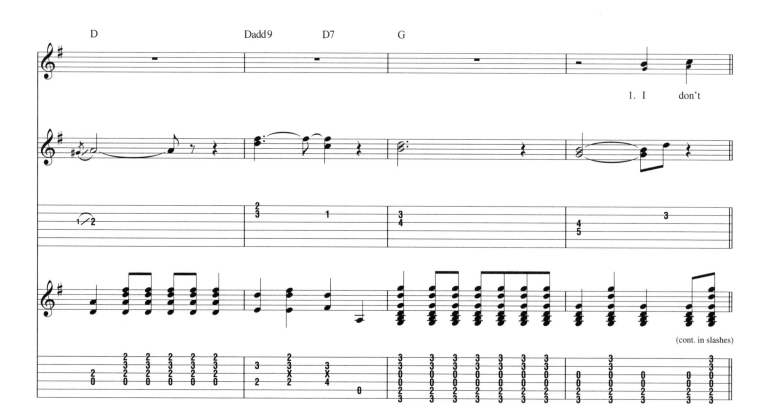

up while I'm gone ___ please let me know. _____

Guitar Solo

Verse

Gtr. 2: w/ Rhy. Fig. 1

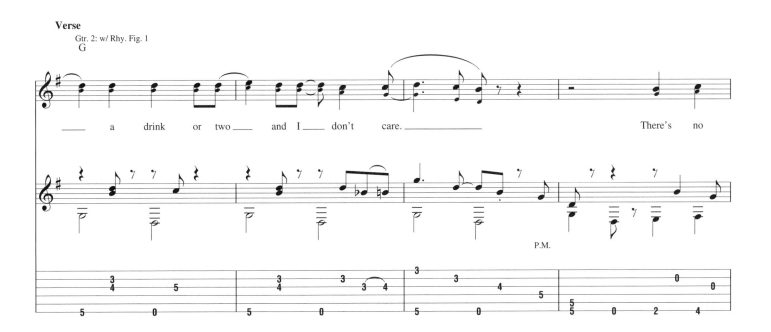

_____ a drink or two _____ and I _____ don't care. _____ There's no

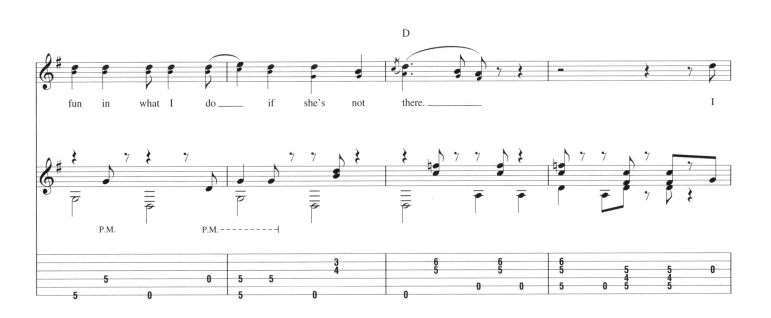

fun in what I do _____ if she's not there. _____ I

Bkgd. Vocs.: w/ Voc. Fig. 1

won-der what_ went wrong? _ I've wait-ed far_ too long. _ But I

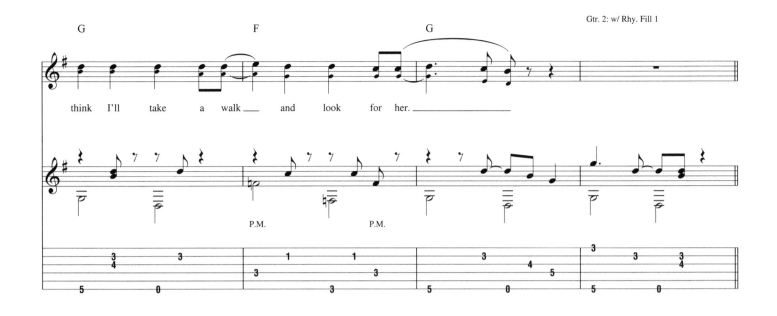

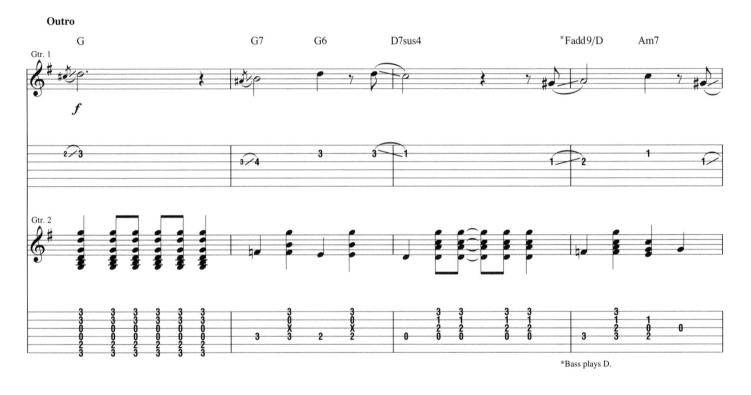

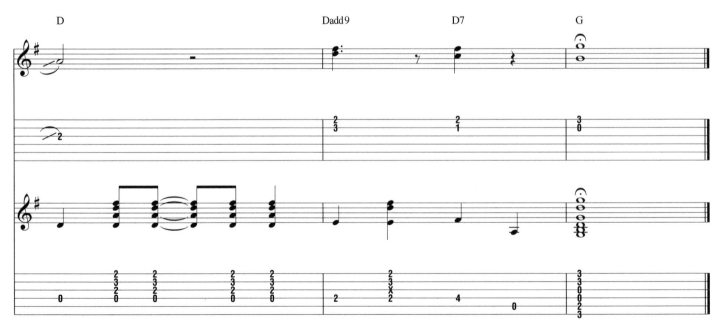

What You're Doing

Words and Music by John Lennon and Paul McCartney

*John Lennon
**George Harrison

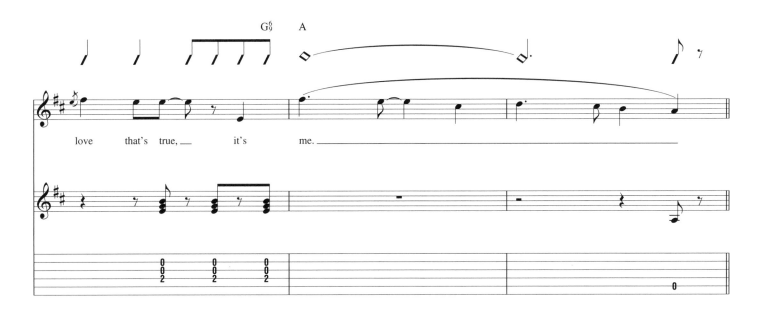

love that's true, __ it's me. _____

Verse

Gtr. 1: w/ Fill 1
Gtr. 2: w/ Rhy. Fig. 1

Gtr. 1: w/ Riff A

3., 4. Please stop your ly-in', you've got me cry-in', girl. __ Why should it

To Coda ⊕

Chorus

1st time, Gtrs. 1 & 2: w/ Rhy. Figs. 2 & 2A
2nd time, Gtrs. 1 & 2: w/ Rhy. Figs. 2 & 2A (1st 2 meas.)
1st time, Bkgd. Vocs.: w/ Voc. Fig. 1
2nd time, Bkgd. Vocs.: w/ Voc. Fig. 1 (1st 2 meas.)

be so much __ to ask of you, __ what you're do-in' to __ me? __

Guitar Solo

Gtr. 2: w/ Rhy. Fig. 1

*George Harrison

Coda

do - in'   to ___ me.
Oo.) ___

Everybody's Trying to Be My Baby

Words and Music by Carl Lee Perkins

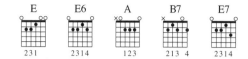

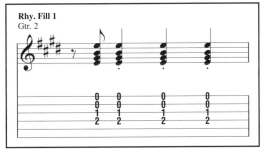

To Coda 1
To Coda 2
B7
A
E
E7
- ry - bod - y's try - ing to be my ba - by now.
let ring
1/2
Guitar Solo
E
Rhy. Fig. 2
let ring
A
E
let ring
D.S. al Coda 1
B7
A
E
End Rhy. Fig. 2
3. Went
let ring

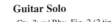

⊕ Coda 1

Guitar Solo
Gtr. 2: w/ Rhy. Fig. 2 (2 times)

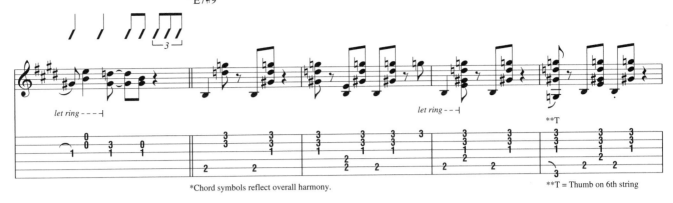

*Chord symbols reflect overall harmony.

**T = Thumb on 6th string

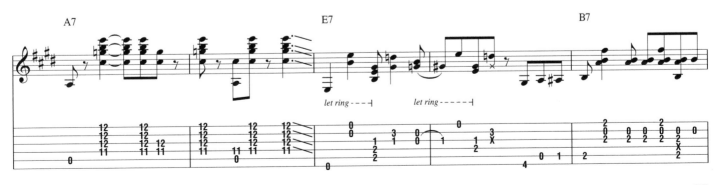

GUITAR NOTATION LEGEND

Guitar music can be notated three different ways: on a *musical staff*, in *tablature*, and in *rhythm slashes*.

RHYTHM SLASHES are written above the staff. Strum chords in the rhythm indicated. Use the chord diagrams found at the top of the first page of the transcription for the appropriate chord voicings. Round noteheads indicate single notes.

THE MUSICAL STAFF shows pitches and rhythms and is divided by bar lines into measures. Pitches are named after the first seven letters of the alphabet.

TABLATURE graphically represents the guitar fingerboard. Each horizontal line represents a string, and each number represents a fret.

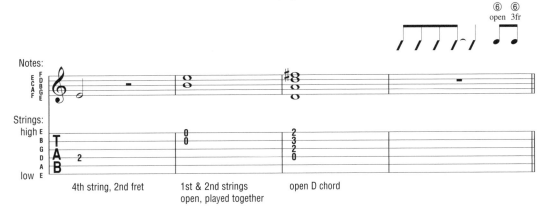

4th string, 2nd fret

1st & 2nd strings open, played together

open D chord

Definitions for Special Guitar Notation

HALF-STEP BEND: Strike the note and bend up 1/2 step.

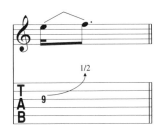

WHOLE-STEP BEND: Strike the note and bend up one step.

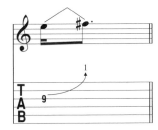

GRACE NOTE BEND: Strike the note and immediately bend up as indicated.

SLIGHT (MICROTONE) BEND: Strike the note and bend up 1/4 step.

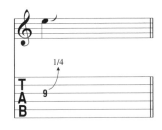

BEND AND RELEASE: Strike the note and bend up as indicated, then release back to the original note. Only the first note is struck.

PRE-BEND: Bend the note as indicated, then strike it.

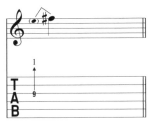

PRE-BEND AND RELEASE: Bend the note as indicated. Strike it and release the bend back to the original note.

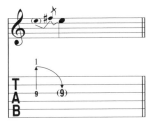

UNISON BEND: Strike the two notes simultaneously and bend the lower note up to the pitch of the higher.

VIBRATO: The string is vibrated by rapidly bending and releasing the note with the fretting hand.

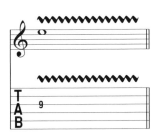

WIDE VIBRATO: The pitch is varied to a greater degree by vibrating with the fretting hand.

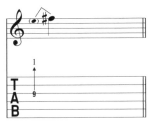

HAMMER-ON: Strike the first (lower) note with one finger, then sound the higher note (on the same string) with another finger by fretting it without picking.

PULL-OFF: Place both fingers on the notes to be sounded. Strike the first note and without picking, pull the finger off to sound the second (lower) note.

LEGATO SLIDE: Strike the first note and then slide the same fret-hand finger up or down to the second note. The second note is not struck.

SHIFT SLIDE: Same as legato slide, except the second note is struck.

TRILL: Very rapidly alternate between the notes indicated by continuously hammering on and pulling off.

TAPPING: Hammer ("tap") the fret indicated with the pick-hand index or middle finger and pull off to the note fretted by the fret hand.

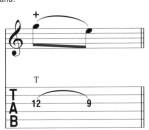

NATURAL HARMONIC: Strike the note while the fret-hand lightly touches the string directly over the fret indicated.

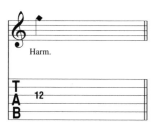

PINCH HARMONIC: The note is fretted normally and a harmonic is produced by adding the edge of the thumb or the tip of the index finger of the pick hand to the normal pick attack.

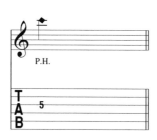

HARP HARMONIC: The note is fretted normally and a harmonic is produced by gently resting the pick hand's index finger directly above the indicated fret (in parentheses) while the pick hand's thumb or pick assists by plucking the appropriate string.

PICK SCRAPE: The edge of the pick is rubbed down (or up) the string, producing a scratchy sound.

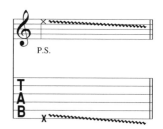

MUFFLED STRINGS: A percussive sound is produced by laying the fret hand across the string(s) without depressing, and striking them with the pick hand.

PALM MUTING: The note is partially muted by the pick hand lightly touching the string(s) just before the bridge.

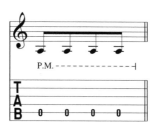

RAKE: Drag the pick across the strings indicated with a single motion.

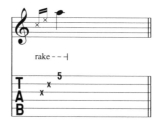

TREMOLO PICKING: The note is picked as rapidly and continuously as possible.

ARPEGGIATE: Play the notes of the chord indicated by quickly rolling them from bottom to top.

VIBRATO BAR DIVE AND RETURN: The pitch of the note or chord is dropped a specified number of steps (in rhythm), then returned to the original pitch.

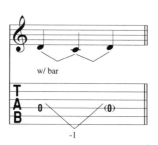

VIBRATO BAR SCOOP: Depress the bar just before striking the note, then quickly release the bar.

VIBRATO BAR DIP: Strike the note and then immediately drop a specified number of steps, then release back to the original pitch.

Additional Musical Definitions

 *(accent)* • Accentuate note (play it louder).

(accent) • Accentuate note with great intensity.

(staccato) • Play the note short.

⊓ • Downstroke

V • Upstroke

D.S. al Coda • Go back to the sign (𝄋), then play until the measure marked "*To Coda*," then skip to the section labelled "**Coda**."

D.C. al Fine • Go back to the beginning of the song and play until the measure marked "*Fine*" (end).

Rhy. Fig. • Label used to recall a recurring accompaniment pattern (usually chordal).

Riff • Label used to recall composed, melodic lines (usually single notes) which recur.

Fill • Label used to identify a brief melodic figure which is to be inserted into the arrangement.

Rhy. Fill • A chordal version of a Fill.

tacet • Instrument is silent (drops out).

• Repeat measures between signs.

• When a repeated section has different endings, play the first ending only the first time and the second ending only the second time.

NOTE: Tablature numbers in parentheses mean:
1. The note is being sustained over a system (note in standard notation is tied), or
2. The note is sustained, but a new articulation (such as a hammer-on, pull-off, slide or vibrato) begins, or
3. The note is a barely audible "ghost" note (note in standard notation is also in parentheses).

GUITAR RECORDED VERSIONS®

Guitar Recorded Versions® are note-for-note transcriptions of guitar music taken directly off recordings. This series, one of the most popular in print today, features some of the greatest guitar players and groups from blues and rock to country and jazz.

Guitar Recorded Versions are transcribed by the best transcribers in the business. Every book contains notes and tablature. Visit www.halleonard.com for our complete selection.

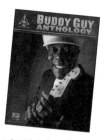

RECORDED VERSIONS GUITAR®

AUTHENTIC TRANSCRIPTIONS WITH NOTES AND TABLATURE

FOR MORE INFORMATION, SEE YOUR LOCAL MUSIC DEALER, OR WRITE TO:

HAL•LEONARD® CORPORATION

7777 W. BLUEMOUND RD. P.O. BOX 13819 MILWAUKEE, WI 53213

Complete songlists and more at www.halleonard.com
Prices, contents, and availability subject to change without notice.

1110